UHSM Academy Library

R00154A4989

One Thought to Be Taken Once a Day

~~~

366 Well-Being Thoughts for Health Professionals

Emma Allende

BALBOA
PRESS
A DIVISION OF HAY HOUSE

BF ALL

Copyright © 2012 by Emma Allende.

All rights reserved. No part of this book may be used or reproduced by any means, graphic, electronic, or mechanical, including photocopying, recording, taping or by any information storage retrieval system without the written permission of the publisher except in the case of brief quotations embodied in critical articles and reviews.

ISBN: 978-1-4525-6352-7 (sc)
ISBN: 978-1-4525-6353-4 (e)
ISBN: 978-1-4525-6354-1 (hc)

Library of Congress Control Number: 2012921773

Balboa Press books may be ordered through booksellers or by contacting:
Balboa Press
A Division of Hay House
1663 Liberty Drive
Bloomington, IN 47403
www.balboapress.com
1-(877) 407-4847

Because of the dynamic nature of the Internet, any web addresses or links contained in this book may have changed since publication and may no longer be valid. The views expressed in this work are solely those of the author and do not necessarily reflect the views of the publisher, and the publisher hereby disclaims any responsibility for them.

The author of this book does not dispense medical advice or prescribe the use of any technique as a form of treatment for physical, emotional, or medical problems without the advice of a physician, either directly or indirectly. The intent of the author is only to offer information of a general nature to help you in your quest for emotional and spiritual well-being. In the event you use any of the information in this book for yourself, which is your constitutional right, the author and the publisher assume no responsibility for your actions.

Any people depicted in stock imagery provided by Thinkstock are models, and such images are being used for illustrative purposes only. Certain stock imagery © Thinkstock.

Printed in the United States of America

Balboa Press rev. date: 11/27/12

Introduction

If you are reading this, then there must be some reason why this book has brought your attention. "One Thought To Be Taken Once A Day" has been created for people who like you have felt attracted somehow by it. Maybe by the title, maybe by the story behind the author or by some other still unknown reason. If you think you have come across this book by chance, think twice. What's inside yourself that attracted you to it?

I wouldn't like to suggest that it is possible this book will help you to work through some of the less than easy challenges in your role as a health professional, being more in charge of your own life while helping you to grow towards self actualization.

It is well known that health professionals experience high levels of stress, making them more prone to suffer from high blood pressure, ulcers, cancer and even early deaths. This has a tremendous impact on patient care.

This book will teach you how to keep your core self protected while juggling the demands of job and life.

Just take one thought once a day and absorb its therapeutic effect.

One Thought to Be Taken Once a Day

1. *Caring about my staff with love will help me to understand myself better.*

2. *I care about optimising my relationship with my colleagues. I'm asking myself "What has to be true for this person to react like that?" "What kind of thoughts this person must have in order to react like that?" "What does he believe about himself?" This helps me to understand my colleagues.*

3. *There is something within me that pushes me to transcend. Sharing my knowledge will make me somehow immortal. I decide to share my knowledge openly with the new generations of staff and I'm starting to notice what the benefits are for me too.*

4.   *What makes me happy or sad is my mind. Today I will focus on thinking happy thoughts and hopeful thoughts for myself, my patients and my staff.*

5.   *Sometimes all that your patient needs is a "human being", not a "human doing" who is so busy who can't establish eye contact or a "human having" full of qualifications. And... yes, of course, you can be the three of them.*

6.   *I like to promote my patient's intuition too so they can help me more with the diagnoses and description of the effects the medication has in their bodies.*

7. *Stress maintained over time raises cortisol levels suppressing the ability of the body to repair itself. By taking care of my mental health I can do something to be in control of my cortisol levels.*

8. *Changing how you feel about something will shift automatically your behaviour. Did you know you get to choose how you feel about things?*

9. *There's no such a thing as a bad day I'm just having another opportunity to grow while learning. I love getting feedback from my bad days. How good are my bad days!*

10. *Without my thoughts my world wouldn't exit. What would I like to create with my thoughts today? A happy experience or a bad one?*

11. *All my colleagues are doing the best they know and can with what it is available to them at any moment in time. That includes me too.*

12. *Next time you see a patient pay attention to your energy. Does your energy go up or down? Do you feel anything in your heart? Do you feel uplifted or constricted? Do you feel a connection with him? And try to modify you energy around the situation. You could be very pleasantly surprised to discover new things you didn't know before.*

13. *Give someone a hug; you'll be stimulating the growth hormone that contributes to stimulate the immune system, balances blood pressure and settles the mood.*

14. *I educate my patients about how they have to listen to their bodies and trust what the body has to say to them in order to cooperate in the healing of the illness.*

15. *I've realised that to overcome fear I have to become calm to allow courage to neutralise it. I become calm by focusing in my gentle breathing.*

16. *Today while I'm having a break at work I choose to enjoy slowly my coffee and as I start feeling good I say nice things about my colleagues. I observe what impact this makes to my life. I never thought something so simple could be so powerful.*

17. *When one of the parts of my body is painful, I focus on which other parts of my body are working well. This removes my obsession with my symptoms and allows my immune system to do its job.*

18. *I recognize that my patients have their own boundaries and they are to be respected. I ask politely before any procedure and calibrate the body language as well as listening to what my patient has to say. I observe how their words and body language are a match.*

19. *It's becoming easier for me to recognize when I'm angry and I look for positive ways I can think of to express it in different more positive ways.*

20. *I allow myself to adapt well to the changes in my department.*

21. *It's the thoughts and beliefs which make the difference between a bad behaviour and a good one. What kind of thoughts would I allow my mind to have?*

22.   *When I feel I don't want something I don't tend to use negative words to describe it. Instead I choose what I want out of it and suddenly I start to see myself talking positive words about a situation that was previously negative.*

23.   *My thinking is determinant of how I present myself to the world. How do I wish people to see me?*

24.   *When I choose my food wisely, it gives me the gift of nourishment. The growth and well being of my cells depend on the energy healthy food provides. In the same way I choose healthy thoughts to feed my mind. A healthy thought is the one that keeps in harmony with who I really am. Nobody needs to know what I think. I can decide if I want to share my thoughts or not with others.*

25. *I may not be aware how sometimes I allow other people's fears to get into me. When I feel scared I first check inside if those fears are the product of someone who said something to me or if they are my own real fears. If they are not mine, would I hold onto them?*

26. *As I feel compassion for myself, my fears start to vanish.*

27. *I am much more than just my fears.*

28. *Engage in meaningful conversations as they help to keep the limbic system in balance.*

29. *In order to deal with illness is useful to connect with the energetic emotional components of the illness. It is good to ask questions although the may seem unusual. So for example in the case that the illness would have had a purpose in my life I would ask myself "What would that be?" I remain in silence to allow the answer to emerge from within. Once I find the purpose "what would I offer to the illness to fulfill that purpose?" "Is it perhaps loving myself more or decreasing the amount of work that I do?"....*

30. *My eyes see what my mind has known before. Sometimes I have to believe something first in order to see it later on. It's not all about seeing it to be able to believe it.*

31. *There's a reason for me being here in this world and alive. When I seem to forget about what the reason is, I keep my mind quiet and observe my thoughts flowing. Just observing them, not feeling them. When my mind becomes quieter suddenly a more positive thought comes up to the surface. I follow it and I give it my full attention. That's life starting to tell me what I already knew and forgot for a while.*

32. *It is good to like thinking the thoughts you are thinking, so you would distinguish the helpful thoughts from the not so helpful ones.*

33. *When I blend my rational mind with my intuition, I have access to much more information about my patients.*

34. *Whatever I wish to receive from my staff, that's exactly what I have to offer to them.*

35. *There's a subtle energy field around our bodies, we feel warm, cold, drained , light headed ...... It's called bio energy. Once we learn to perceive it, it helps understand how our patients are feeling and how their body is functioning. Combining this with our rational mind we become better health professionals.*

36. *By deciding to feel a bit better now I get an indication that I am already on the road to feeling very good soon. This gives me reassurance that better things are coming and I'm on the right track.*

37. *Everyday at the hospital we pick up different energies from different emotions from patients and staff. By cleaning our energy in between patients we don't pass the emotional state from one bed to the next one in the ward.*

38. *Some ideas about how to clean our energy are: Applying peripheral vision, paying close attention and purposefully feeling the water running down our hands while we wash them, grounding ourselves in every step on the floor and prolonging the breathing out.*

39. *A good start of the day at the hospital begins at home as soon as I get up when I decide on purpose to think helpful thoughts.*

40. *Today I decide I'm going to talk about something inspiring with my colleagues during the break at work and observe how they reenergise as a consequence of it.*

41. *Our bodies are made of atoms that arrange themselves and make cells and organs. We are energy and our emotions are energy in motion.*

42. *When things are changing at work, I remember and reassure myself that it's just change ,this helps me to remain calm and can be an opportunity for me to grow and change too. I like to write down how many ways I can think for me to start to enjoy the process of changing.*

43. *If it's dark I turn on the light. If there's fear I turn on love. When I feel scared I start by thinking what I love around me. That includes even the smallest things like "I love the chair I'm sitting on because is comfortable or I love the fact that I'm wearing clothes that keep me warm...." I keep doing this on purpose for a few seconds or minutes and I observe how fear vanishes. Fear and Love cannot coexist together.*

44. *When I feel stuck inside my own circle of safety I embrace uncertainty. This way it makes easier to push my own boundaries.*

45. *I'm determined to make life a perpetual thrive.*

46. *When I wish to know what kind of health service is delivered I observe how the staff get on with each other. If they look energetic, happy in their jobs and with an open attitude there's a greater chance that they would be delivering good care.*

47. *There may be times when you find difficult to trust your staff. In the same way, you may wonder how easy it is to trust yourself and …..as you are now reading this you may realise that you knew all along you had all the resources needed to solve any problems that may arise at work. By trusting yourself, trusting your staff wouldn't be an issue anymore.*

48. *There are only a few real emergencies. Stop worrying about having many patients waiting for you. Dedicate a brief time to restore yourself, so your clinic starts flowing easily and effortlessly.*

49. *When we argue "I'm right, you are wrong! " Who is doubting more about himself and feeling vulnerable? We can shout out loud and still never be right. If one of us was really right there wouldn't be a need for shouting, we would only need to whisper.*

50. *Remember that being scared of developing a mental illness is just a sign of anxiety. It doesn't constitute mental illness just by itself.*

51. *Dedicating time to the basic needs of your body keeps the chemicals in your brain under balance.*

52. *The best asset a hospital can have is a mentally and physically healthy staff who are happy in their jobs.*

53. *Ask the patients what's their "gut feeling" about the illness and you'll be surprised how much information comes to the surface.*

54. *The release of histamine is directly related to an asthma attack. Now guess which one is the neurotransmitter that gets released under the emotion of fear? As you are reading this now ....how many other ways can you think of to prevent an asthma attack from happening?*

55. *Ask yourself what would be the cost of holding that negative belief? Is it worth it?*

56. *Your brain is like a computer. It's got its own software and of course its own recycle bin. Declutter your brain in the same way you declutter your computer and recycle your thoughts.*

57. *In any life event either you win or you learn and by learning you end up winning anyway.*

58. *Remember that you can always choose to act from a place of loving your job instead of a place of obligation.*

59. *The best medical equipment would not fulfil its potential unless it is in the hands of someone who is eager to use it and enthusiastic and hopeful of being successful.*

60. *Would you like a better future? Then you have to stop wishing your past would have been different.*

61. *Some illnesses are more common depending on our life styles and our life styles depend on our thoughts and our thoughts depend on us. Isn't it simpler than you thought it was?*

62. *Replace "I can't "with "There may be a change I could". When I could, "How would I know that?" I perhaps could do it and I don't know it just yet".*

63. *Replace the word "problem" with the word "challenge". Which one is more empowering ?*

64. *Do you suffer from food intolerance or other allergies? Histamine is released in your body in an allergic reaction. Histamine is also released when you allow the emotion of fear to take over you.*

65. *Start watching your thoughts and begin to notice your thought patterns. Are they helpful? Being aware of your thoughts is the first step to move toward a more supportive thinking.*

66. *Do you often find yourself refusing to think something nice about yourself? OK, now try it the other way round and refuse to think something bad about yourself.*

67. *Make a conscious decision to live your life in the proximity of hope. Soon you'll see how happy things come your way and the previous struggles seem to disappear in the distance.*

68. *There are more versions of the reality than the one you are experiencing. Once you learn to see them you can choose which one you want to adopt.*

69. *Listen to how your patient describes his symptoms in his own vocabulary and ask yourself "How can I communicate better with this patient and put him first?" He will perceive this and the rapport will be established at a deeper level.*

70. *People who are exposed to greenery have lower blood pressure and better mood when compared with people working in windowless rooms.*

71. *You are much more than just your thoughts you are thinking right now.*

72. *Dedicate everyday at least 10 minutes purposefully to think about what you would like to happen in your life.*

73. *Remember the first time someone bullied you and how it can be related to how you behave now. Remind yourself of all the resources you own inside to choose more adaptive and beneficial ways to react. Do you still want to bully that person now? Who would be losing after all? How could you really win?*

74. *The EEG signals detected from the brain of people listening to music and the ones just imagining music are indistinguishable. What would you dare to imagine today?*

75. *You are always on time to change the perception about yourself and about the world around you.*

76. *Start by loving yourself. The rest becomes easier. Once you change your attitude towards yourself, loving your patients will come automatically.*

77. *You are a miracle, in order for you to be reading this today all your ancestors had to live at least up to reproductive age. Can you see how important you are?*

78. *Look around you. The things you see didn't exist at some point, apart from being a single thought that someone held. What would you like to think of that could become a reality?*

79. *Many little acts of kindness for your patients will bring you a life full of kindness for yourself.*

80. *We are not as individual as we think we are. We are all connected at a molecular level and at emotional level.*

81. *Look at the way you talk to yourself. Are you your best friend or your worst enemy?*

82. *What I think about myself is what it really matters and this will be reflected in my actions. What others think about me doesn't have any power over me unless I give it that permission.*

83. *Any emotional state lasts less than 60 seconds. If it keeps longer it is because we keep adding logs to the fire, entertaining the same thought repeating it inside our heads. What thought would we like to entertain?*

84. *Emotional states are catching. Are yours worth being contagious?*

85. *Dare to treat your colleagues nicely and do good things to them. You can do it directly or in a way they'll never find out, watch them grow and see how you grow even more.*

86. *I am in charge of my mind; I can stop my mind using me. I am in charge of the involuntary thoughts processes as I can address them despite being involuntary.*

87. *Today make your intent to focus on positive and good things. Once you start doing this on purpose notice how you start to love your new becoming happier life.*

88. *When I look at my patients, I try to see that behind every single face there's a story. Whatever the story is I give it full consideration. Everybody has a role and a purpose in this life. When I can't find anything interesting in the story I change my point of focus. I look at the positive aspects of the story and what they represent in the overall picture.*

89. *When you are angry and you feel like shouting, start singing the words. This way you can still release the same energy while noticing how the impulse diminishes. You can sing the words inside your head, nobody will notice it. When one shouts there's no thinking, just an impulse. When one sings the brain operates in a different way.*

90. *Repetitive experiences induce neurogenesis. Guess what repetitive thoughts that are followed by repetitive behaviours do.....*

91.   *By relaxing yourself you'll help your body to reduce the inflammatory processes as the cortisol levels decrease and you also give a break to your immune system allowing it to recover and be strong for any possible infections to come. Relax and you will not get so many colds.*

92.   *You can associate pain or pleasure to your thoughts. Choose what kind of thoughts you want to be associated with what kind of feeling.*

93.   *One of the purposes of sleep is to allow your body to recover. Don't underestimate the power of sleep specially when you work on shifts and make sure you make it a priority. Your patients deserve a well rested doctor, nurse......So you do too.*

94. *Today is not just another day, it is a gift given to you to be surprised and amazed at how much good you can deliver today.*

95. *Reduce sugar intake and caffeine intake in your diet and you'll see how much easier it is to feel in control of your emotions.*

96. *Sometimes it's easier to make problems larger than smaller because we find safety in our recurrent patterns of thinking. By daring to slightly move your thinking to something that makes you feel slightly better you push your boundaries further away form your safety circle and expand your thinking, reducing this way your levels of anxiety.*

97. *Under the emotion of fear your body releases cortisol and spend it in the fight flight response. Cortisol is an important natural anti-inflammatory substance. If you waste the cortisol in the fight flight response the remaining cortisol is not used on the inflammatory processes of your body, therefore you are more prone to develop inflammatory diseases like rheumatoid arthritis.*

98. *Have you been feeling quite low and angry recently? Try to stop listening to the news and or reading the newspapers for a couple of weeks and see what difference that makes to your mood and your whole life. By the way, don't worry as you will still be informed. It will just happen in a different way.*

99. *Did you know that when you look at fears closely, they vanish? Any emotion lasts around 45-60 seconds. If you hold and hug the fear it will vanish. However it will keep going for longer if you keep igniting it with your thoughts.*

100. *In how many ways can you reach people to make a difference in their lives?*

101. *Smiling releases endorphins even when you fake it.*

102. *Children see, children do. Staff sees, staff does. Careful with your behaviour when you are with your trainees. Where you bullied at the hospital? Don't pass it to the next generation.*

103. *"What's in it for me?" Is this what rules your life? What about if you didn't know what's in it for you? What about if you only knew that there was something good in it waiting for you but you really didn't know what that was? That way you would be opening new possibilities of good things happening to you. Try it and test it yourself.*

104. *We all do best by taken good care of ourselves and those around us. You are creating your safety circle around you when you care about your colleagues at work.*

105. *Emotions spread quickly, clean yourself with good thoughts for at least 5 minutes after being exposed to viral emotions and don't forget to cover your mouth when you sneeze negative thoughts.*

106. *Change your project if things are not going too well, but never abandon your ultimate goal.*

107. *Giving comes natural and releases endorphins. If you live your life from a point of scarcity it doesn't feel good and that is because you are going against your true nature of sharing.*

108. *There is decreased activity in the medial prefrontal and posterior cingulate cortex in people who meditate regularly regardless of the type of meditation they do as connecting with your inner being activates the same neuropathways. Spending just 10 minutes in silence each day can change your life.*

109. *We relate with our environment by exchanging energy through breathing and by eating energy through food. Make a good relationship with the food you eat, and pay attention to how your food is making you feel while you eat it. If it's not a positive feeling probably there's not a good exchange in energy. Try to feel how your food nourishes every cell in your body, listen to your body.*

110. *Your patient is much more than the physical body presented in front of you. Remember to offer something to the spiritual part of your patients too, not only the physical part. It doesn't take a lot of effort and improves your patient's immune system and your own. Offer a smile for free.*

111. *No matter if you don't believe your patient has a chance of recovery. Just by considering it, your body language will change and you'll be in a better position to offer reassurance and comfort.*

112. *If you dedicate a lot of time to think a thought, it may become a belief. Is that belief one you want to keep?*

113. *If you slow down your breathing, your feelings slow down too.*

114. *Can you smile with your eyes?*

115. *Fight –Flight response muscles are located in the neck and lower back. This is the origin of those unspecific headaches, neck and back pain.*

116. *Stay in this present moment. What do you see now? What do you hear now? What do you smell and taste? What do you feel and where do you feel it? In what part of your body?*

117. *The foods you eat contribute to your mind body balance.*

118. *If you've been labelled as being too sensitive for being a doctor, nurse......... congratulations! That means your nervous system is more alert and you perceive things much quicker than others. Such an important diagnostic skill to have when combined with your medical knowledge.*

119. *What was it in your childhood that you were curious about? You can still be...... curious. Curiosity is the door to personal growth.*

120. *Trust that everything is perfect. It really is, you just can't see it now. Trust.*

121. *In difficult clinical circumstances, just by speaking, you may not express all you want to say. You may feel as if you have to squeeze feelings into the limitations of language. If you feel like that in front of a patient, stop talking and allow your brain to direct your body to the proper body language attached to your feelings. Your patient will know what you want to say. Align with your feelings before saying anything to your patients, particularly bad news.*

122. *The word "Healing" in a medical environment can sound a bit weird, but we don't get surprised when we talk about "wound healing". Maybe is time to allow the "Healing" word to expand far beyond and use it more. Cancer healing , body healing, mind healing, diabetes healing, asthma healing......*

123. *Some people say: "I can't believe it unless I see it". Medicine is not the same as maths and every patient is a different world. Sometimes, if you believe it before you see it, you start looking for new and different possibilities that you didn't consider before and that can make a different outcome to a clinical case.*

124. *Intuition is a very important part of yourself. Through your intuitive abilities you have access to much more information about your patient than just by asking the protocol questions. Intuition can be a very useful tool before you prescribe something for your patient when combined with your medical knowledge.*

125. *Look around you and write down in what good way every single member of your team contributes to it.*

126. *Don't forget that nature provides you with everything your body needs. This potentiates the healing power of your body. If you feel you are running out of energy, put nature on your side. Go out for a walk. Start drinking green smoothies etc...*

127. *It can give you a lot of insight if you check inside yourself how you are feeling and what you are thinking. Do this several times throughout the day at least as often as you check your mobile phone.*

128. *When you look at your computer screen, you are applying foveal vision, that's associated with the fight and flight response and anxiety, same thing when you use a microscope. Social skills are more associated with peripheral vision. As a doctor you have to combine little breaks from foveal vision and apply peripheral vision throughout the day to balance your brain.*

129. *Forgiveness allows you to be free from the expectations you may have held of others. When you forgive, you don't do it for them, you do it as a present for yourself to release the negative emotion the other person left in you and become free. When you forgive someone you don't have to tell them if you don't want. It's an internal process.*

130. *Autumn suits you. Pick up the fruitful thoughts and just allow your negative ones drop as the leaves from the tree........to allow time for renewal.*

131. *You cannot be a human being for others unless you first become a human being for yourself.*

132. *If you don't offer unconditional love to your patients you are missing some of the most powerful healing tools.*

133. *Perhaps you would like to know that life can't forget about you, it caresses you with the wind. Remember that when it's windy.*

134. *There are many correct ways for the patient to feel about his illness.*

135. *Dreams become reality. Would you like an example? In 1854 Kelule was dozing on a double decker bus and dreamt about atoms all around him and felt he had to organize them. When he woke up he decided to make model atoms joining balls with sticks. Don't underestimate your dreams. Thanks to this we understand atoms much better.*

136. *Fear of having a heart attack can just be fear and not the attack itself and that comes out of anxiety.*

137. *Christmas is about believing not about seeing. Give yourself a chance and think of the song. I wish it could be Christmas everyday.*

138. *An emergency can present at any time. You may not have full control about what happens to you but you definitely have the power to choose how you react to what is presented to you.*

139. *Look for your real power inside yourself. There's a much bigger part inside you and that's who you really are. Start listening to your inner being.*

140. *Once you realize you are complete you can't envy or be jealous of anyone because nothing has been taken away from you as you have it all inside. Once you realise about this you'll achieve much more than you thought before.*

141. *Just for a minute stop, listen to your breathing and notice the ratio between your inhale and exhale, prolong your exhale until your body brings the inhale on its own. Observe how deep you can breathe. Repeat this a few times and observe how you calm down.*

142. *There's only two ways you can feel about a situation: good or bad. Check within yourself several times a day how you feel about every situation and look for ways to move gradually from bad to good. While you are at the hospital make your dominant intent to feel peaceful while you work. You deserve it, your patients deserve it, your colleagues deserve it.*

143. *Are your thoughts limiting you or disempowering you? Change them.*

144. *It doesn't really matter what anyone thinks about you as long as you act from a place of unconditional love.*

145. *Sometimes when we look at other people who are happy we feel threatened by them as we may feel we haven't reached that happiness ourselves or we don't know how to get it. Don't forget that the happy person was just like you at some point, unknown, disoriented, like anyone else. He is no danger and remember that joy is contagious if you allow it to be.*

146. *You are in charge of the way people treat you at work. By changing your behaviour you change what people see in you and you offer to them a different attitude to interact with.*

147. *Opportunities to expand on your career start to appear once you allow yourself to expand personally.*

148. *Go beyond practicing your five senses and use your sixth sense (intuition) too. Tune in your intuition, in this specific time and space, in this moment and notice how that affects your breathing rhythm.*

149. *It's been demonstrated that negative experiences affect neuroplasticity. Positive experiences too but in an opposite way.*

150. *Don't act if you feel anxious, give yourself at least 45 secs. In some emergencies you can still let yourself have 45 secs for yourself to allow your thinking to settle and come up with solutions.*

151. *You can think that problems give you a hard time or that problems are opportunities for growth. Learn from them and from this point of thinking problems are easier to deal with. How can your problem be something good that adds new learnings to your life?*

152. *Are you highly intuitive? You are a very valuable member of staff and it's good to have someone in the team with an early warning system, so important when you work in healthcare.*

153. *Your body sends messages about what you think and you are not consciously aware of it. Listen to your body and your patient's bodies.*

154. *You will stop envying your colleagues once you dedicate time daily to write things you have achieved in a notebook even if they seem insignificant like "I can ride a bike" , "I can walk", or "I can read and write". Engage in a daily practice of writing your successes in a notebook. No matter how small they are.*

155. *Feel the energy of anxiety in your body. Imagine it as a cloud of moving energy and perceive where it's located in your body. Now push that cloud up, up, up leaving your body reaching the sky and observe how it dissolves in the sky.*

156. *When you meditate, the flow of racing thoughts decreases gradually until it stops and you get to experience an empty peaceful mind.*

157. *Give yourself 5 minutes a day to meditate and think that "All is well" even if it seems it's not true. By thinking "All is well" you'll calm down all those racing apparently uncontrollable thoughts, allowing more self supporting thoughts to come to surface.*

158. *Fear of fainting can just be the emotion of fear without any evidence and could come due to high levels of anxiety.*

159. *It is up to you if you want to choose a thought that is supportive or a thought that is demoralizing.*

160. *Fell anxious? Can't breathe? Place both hands over your heart and keep them there paying attention to all different sensations arising. In less than a minute you'll feel better and you'll notice how your breathing pattern shifts.*

161. *Have big expectations for yourself, as you tend to become what you think about.*

162. *When you feel out of balance please don't take any action as this is not the right time. First take care of yourself and once you are in balance, action will flow in the right direction easily and effortlessly.*

163. *Chronic depression is linked to chronic thoughts in the same way that chronic happiness is linked to chronic thoughts. Start to think more of the kind of thoughts you like and enjoy. Think thoughts that are helpful to you and make them chronic habits.*

164. *Have positive expectations of every single member of your staff. Soon you'll see how they become what you expected from them as they will feel comfort in the knowing that someone believes they can do better and that ignites rockets of desire to improve.*

165. *When I am full of good I can give it to my patients and the staff around me.*

166. *I can learn from my patients as much as they learn from me.*

167. *Get entertained with your dream; you may be amazed to confirm that your life goes well.*

168. *If you are happy and you know it ...."Shout inside" so you can listen to yourself.*

169. *You have the responsibility to decide if you want to change your life or not.*

170. *Switches are made to turn the light on. I can decide when to switch on the power within me.*

171. *Our bodies are perfect. They can also contribute to heal themselves and I like supporting that process in my patients.*

172. *When I argue my blood pressure increases. When I take a deep breath by blood pressure slows down.*

173. *Be careful with deciding to be happy as people may not ignore you anymore.*

174. *Today is my purposeful intention to offer a smile to every single person I meet in the corridor and observe their reaction.*

175. *I keep flowing in the artery of life.*

176. *The sun affects life on earth, affects our mood and our health. If you don't feel at your best go outside and contact nature. This is particularly important if you work inside a theatre and work in a country with not many daylight hours in winter.*

177. *Just by appreciating the small good things as they happen through the day and joining them together, your thinking will gradually shift towards better feeling thoughts. Examples of small things are: the fact that you have clothes to wear, water to drink, people to talk to, heating at home, a bed to sleep etc....*

178. *Pay attention inside to what is important to you.*

179. *We are vibrational beings and emotions go through our body with different physiology changes. When you pay attention to your emotions you become aware about what they do to your body and this is an insightful process.*

180. *Start talking more about what you want to see in your life instead about what you don't want to experience and observe what happens.*

181. *Compassion highlights everybody's face.*

182. *The energy of my patient's emotions is also recorded in an ECG.*

183. *I am able to see my patients as whole beautiful human beings, full of resources inside to contribute to their recovery.*

184. *A little touch of faith makes life worthwhile. Don't be scared of saying you've got faith on something, someone, God, destiny, yourself, the power of the human body to recover.......... It's probably the first step to change your thinking towards founding a solution to that problem you have as you see things from outside the box when you have faith. Apply the power of faith.*

185. *Change inside and observe how the outside changes too.*

186. *Give yourself on purpose 2 good reasons for pursuing your goal for every single one that comes to your mind suggesting that you can't do it. Do this even if you don't believe it at first as you'll activate different neuropathways that you didn't before.*

187. *When I don't know something, I remain at peace as by embracing unknowing I'm still browsing possible solutions.*

188. *You are always in the right place at the right time. In case that you don't believe it, fake it! Then you'll see how you have been able to make that place and that time the right ones. This would help you to find the best of every situation.*

189. *Love the people who hurt you at work, you don't have to tell them, just do it on the inside and thank them for becoming the catalyst of your expansion and growth. They would be surprised as they wouldn't get the annoying reaction they were expecting from you. You won.*

190. *We are energy beings and we have different methods of measuring it, like the electricity on our hearts on an ECG or our magnetic fields in an MRI.*

191. *Do people usually come and talk to you about their lives when you don't know them? Congratulations that's a convincer that you are a very good listener, one of the best abilities you can have when you are a health professional.*

192. *I am no better or worse than anyone else.*

193. *Pay attention to those first thoughts in the morning as you may find clues about how to solve that problem that kept you awake at the beginning of the night.*

194. *Stop now, take a deep breath with a long breathing out and pay attention to what biological rhythms you notice in your body right now.*

195. *We can come to this world with some genetic predisposition, but it is upon ourselves and how we relate to our environment to activate it. It depends on the food we eat, where we live, if we smoke, the contamination in the air, what we drink.... and of course our levels of stress.*

196. *As clinicians sometimes we find less than easy to deal with our own feelings and that prevents us from understanding the emotional side of our patients' illnesses.*

197. *When you develop yourself personally you are more aware of how you behave and feel. This makes you aware of other colleagues' thoughts and emotions and helps you to understand the patients better.*

198. *Sometimes what you call "a problem " is also a solution. Just ask yourself the question. How can this situation be good? ...and be surprised to find out how many other resources appear that you didn't consider before.*

199. *When you learn to feel your patient's body energy you are ready to start multilevel communication. This is particularly important when applied to patients who are in coma.*

200. *Look at others with unconditional appreciation. You are not doing it for them, but for yourself.*

201. *Smile on purpose even if you have to fake it. Once you fake it, you make it. So even if you don't feel like smiling DO IT! Observe how long it takes for your thoughts to change the content gradually to some slightly better feeling one.*

202. *Your mind is like an iceberg, the tip is pointy, sharp and focus (that's your conscious mind).... and underneath under the water, at a deeper level is bigger, powerful but not visible on the surface, although can make the tip to turn upside down (this is your unconscious mind).*

203. *When you feel irritated, stop and say to yourself: What am I thinking right now? Is that a helpful thought? If it's not helpful, decide to change the thought and say "good things are always available to me and can happen at any time and I don't need to know how or when". Immediately check and see if you feel better. Keep practicing that thought throughout the day.*

204. *I love and appreciate all my patients and in the process of doing it, I feel good inside myself and from good only good things can develop.*

205. *Can you recognize your non-linear mind? It's the one that gives you intuitive information (the gut feeling) in the form of flashes, of suddenly knowing, emotional sensations, imagery, memories, kinaesthetic feelings, information that pops up in your brain firmly, clearly and fresh.*

206. *We know establishing rapport with your patients is very important but not as important as establishing rapport with yourself. You have power about what kind of memories you would like to have in the future.*

207. *Practice medicine from a place of goodness, so when you think back after you retire you will be able to enjoy it once more.*

208. *If I throw a stone in a pond it ripples. In the same way my thoughts ripple through other members of staff. I always have the power to decide if I want to throw a stone or not.*

209. *When a problem is presented to me, at the same time the solution is also presented on the inside.*

210. *No matter who I think I am, I am always expanding.*

211. *When you feel as if your clinic is overwhelming, lots of patients , difficult ones etc..... Have a bottle of Lavender oil or Frankincense oil and spread just a few drops on the carpet in the room and observe how your mood lifts ....*

212. *When you work inside a theatre there's not much opportunity to see if there's good weather or bad weather as many theatres don't have windows, but you can decide to bring the sunshine in..... side.*

213. *Stay true to yourself and choose how you want to be around people at work.*

214. *Have a rainbow day today by eating foods of different colours containing different healthy nutrients.*

215. *Predispose yourself to be happy with yourself at all times. Become your best friend.*

216. *Health consists in having an emotional and physical balance as a whole, not only about having healthy organs.*

217. *Be grateful for your patients and wonder.........*
     In how many different ways would the interaction
     with this person enrich my life?

218. *If your thinking terrifies you, remember that*
     you can decide what you want to believe because
     otherwise you wouldn't go beyond your own
     limiting belief.

219. *When I feel good I feel more hopeful for my*
     patients.

220. *Open you eyes and project your heart. Bless your staff and your patients.*

221. *If the weather forecast is rainy for tomorrow that would be tomorrow, not now, don't rain on your own parade.*

222. *Grudges are heavy to hold onto them. When you let them go life flows at work.*

223. *Change can happen in an instant and yes it can also happen in a positive way. What usually takes longer is to decide if you want change to happen.*

224. *When I share my knowledge with others, they share it with me.*

225. *Your patients experience different kinds of hard......ships, also different easy.....shifts.*

226. *Wouldn't the hard....ships sail easily in calm waters?..........That's right.*

227. *Nature takes its own course and I contribute to direct the flow of life.*

228. *If you take action when you feel good, the goodness expands. Similar things happen when you feel bad.*

229. *I listen with love to my patients' bodies messages.*

230. *When you establish rapport with yourself, you don't hide anymore, people notice it and your patients trust you as they perceive the transparency of your thinking.*

231. *When you feel bad and you don't know how to remove yourself from that feeling, start by appreciating the little things in life and start saying to yourself: " thank you for my feet, thank you for my breakfast , thank you for my house... ......"and notice how saying thanks feels in your body. How muscles relax while you feel grateful. Carry on with all those little things you overlook daily and observe how your mood changes.*

232. *My patient's healing is already in process.*

233. *Just today observe yourself how much you are influenced by others, TV, magazines ....and overall, whose approval do you need? Who is actually choosing your thoughts for yourself?*

234. *Every experience I got through with my patients or staff becomes an opportunity for me to heal myself and heal others.*

235. *Don't squeeze the present moment, expand it and be amazed by how much you haven't paid attention to yet.*

236. *Anger is just another emotion. I accept all my emotions and my patient's emotions and I am aware I can choose to express my anger in better ways and places where it may be more appropriate.*

237. *Every single body is wonderful as it contains the uniqueness of the person living in it.*

238. *Our thoughts come from our previous experiences and also from the influence of those around us. In what ways are people around you affecting your thoughts? Is that something you want to happen? Have you chosen that?*

239. *There are always new ways to do something but you'll never find them if you don't consider they may exist.*

240. *Your present and future circumstances tend to be in alignment with what you are thinking now. Dare to choose thoughts of a more positive nature.*

241. *When I criticise my staff I'm showing them what kind of person I am.*

242. *Open your eyes and be amazed at what you see, feel grateful that you actually have eyes. Look at the faces of people you meet as if they are special because they really are.*

243. *My patients are doing the best they can with the resources they have available to them.*

244. *I express bitterness in a healthy way.*

245. *The involuntary mechanisms going on in our bodies are controlled in an unconscious and perfect way.*

246. *The molecular structure of my body is interacting constantly through the energy I offer with the molecular structure of the rest of beings surrounding me.*

247. *All is well. No matter what, just by saying it and thinking it I start to believe that all is well and gradually I observe how things become easier and easier.*

248. *I love to compliment myself when I achieve fulfillment.*

249. *When you don't know what to offer to a patient start by offering a smile to them. Smiles open the door for your knowledge to flow through as they relax you and shift your thinking.*

250. *It's up to you if you open the door to new ways of thinking or if you keep going in circles in your safety net. What will happen if you pass the line of your safety circle? That line is just a very thin one, thinner that you would expect.*

251. *What would happen if someone who suffers from an asthma attack would learn to control the anxiety associated with it? This is something that can be learnt.*

252. *Allow your positive thoughts to flow into your patient's experience and observe how it improves the outcome in the clinical setting.*

253. *Don't resist the receiving of the goodness of happiness. The key to a happy working environment is just that.*

254. *Don't sabotage yourself with your thoughts. Learn to talk to yourself in a nice way and with compassion. You have to be with yourself for the rest of your life.*

255. *I allow myself to recognise how I am feeling about any situation.*

256. *When you feel like a victim you become powerless.*

257. *Don't underestimate your role as a health professional. It's important for your patients to know that they are supported. Just by being a supportive figure for them, you are doing enough to have a significant role in the healing process of your patient, and then just allow your skills to flow and complement that. Don't be hard on yourself.*

258. *It is important to feel satisfied in your job, value even the smallest step forward in your patients as this helps them to know they are in the right direction and appreciated.*

259. *Competition and separateness can only drag you into becoming very individualistic and that is a risk for depression. It also prevents you from having the life the way you would want. Change the way you look at life as you are part of the whole background and you are not alone. Aim to compete with yourself to become more of who you are, don't compete hard with others as it drags your energy away. When you are full of energy is when you take off.*

260. *You can program your brain to achieve the results that you want in life or you can program it to sabotage yourself. Who is in charge of the program? Don't press the autopilot button.*

261. *By expecting your colleagues to grow, you help them to do it. This has a very a powerful effect at an unconscious level and as a pleasant side effect you grow too.*

262. *When you perceive a situation as threatening, there's a region in your brain called Amygdala where the fear emotion starts. It sends impulses to other brain area (Hypothalamus) and from here a shower of hormones is activated cascading throughout the body and all the physiological and physical reactions take place.*

263. *What would you have to believe in order to help your patient to move towards better health? What would your patient have to believe to cope better with his illness?*

264. *My thoughts can become my own prison. I've got the key to open the cell.*

265. *I trust my patients, I trust my staff, I trust myself and I trust life. All together we are a perfect team.*

266. *I let the past go as it's where it belongs. Future hasn't arrived yet. The point where I have power is in the present.*

267. *It's the energy from my heart the one that allows me to create good rapport with my patients. Rapport doesn't come from intellect.*

268. *Feeling stuck is just an illusion as life is constantly moving. Don't stop yourself from flowing with life.*

269. *Bring your attention to your breathing several times throughout the day and as you are doing it, focus on the part of the body that needs to be healed in your patient or in yourself. Notice what you will see or perceive.*

270. *Appreciate the variety and contrast of all the people who surround you. We live in a diverse world. How fantastic that is!*

271. *Breathing is the only autonomic function that can become conscious. We can control our breathing. Breathe out until there's nothing left and allow the diaphragm to reset on its own.*

272. *What would have to be true for my patient for reacting in that way? What kind of thoughts would my patient have in this situation that makes him react in such a way?*

273. *You can not get what you want if you don't expect it to happen.*

274. *Human contact releases oxytocin and this helps you to be more protected against the effects of stress. It's not good to isolate yourself! You can always do some volunteer work, dedicate time and nurture your friendships, greet people at work........Remember you are doing it for others as well as yourself.*

275. *Even though you have to follow the collective thought processes of your department keep some room inside yourself where you honour your own opinions and remain true to your own values.*

276. *Mental imagery or visualization is a useful tool to break an unhelpful emotional state.*

277. *Don't feed negative thoughts as they grow and reproduce themselves very quickly.*

278. *Don't underestimate the placebo effect. Use the power of the thought on your favour.*

279. *What if it happens? ...... What if it happens? .... What if it happens? No matter what you think in these terms, predisposes the "it" to happen. Be careful what the" it" is.*

280. *Bless the situations you don't like or you find difficult to deal with as they wake you up to ask for something different bigger and better to happen.*

281. *Prefrontal cortex is thicker in people who meditate regularly.*

282. *By practising regularly a positive thought your brain gets used to activate the same neuropathway over and over again. This is similar as using the same muscle several times, it gets stronger.*

283. *Compassion allows certain neuropeptides to be released. This is equally beneficial for the person who offers it and for the person who receives it.*

284. *Before you learn something you go through a process of being confused about the subject. Next time you feel confused remember new learnings are on their way.*

285. *Be fully aware of how your thoughts make you feel and develop the skill of choosing the thought that makes you feel slightly better.*

286. *The relaxation response can be activated by imagining happening. Your brain doesn't really distinguish if something is really happening or if it's just imagined. The neuropathways activated are the same ones.*

287. *What would you accomplish if you would make that change today?*

288. *Take care of the quality of your thoughts as what you think most about yourself ends up being true.*

289. *What would you have to believe in order to make a difference in this patient's life right now?*

290. *When you have 2 patients with similar severity but one of them seems to be doing better than the other, check what kind of beliefs your patient has that can make a difference in the outcome.*

291. *We are responsible for our own change; it's time to stop blaming someone else because of our feelings.*

292. *You can change right now as change happens in an instant.*

293. *When do you want to change? Can you change to your next step right now?*

294. *There are two things you can change easier than you thought. One is your feelings about something and the other is the unhelpful behaviours. By changing your thinking you achieve both.*

295. *What you believe about the outcome of a clinical case constitutes the bases within yourself where you would go to look for evidence to match your belief and to support it*

296. *It's not a question of whether you would do it. It's a question of whether you will do it.*

297. *Change will have to be a must if you really want to happen, not the thought that we perhaps have to do it.*

298. *Embrace that chronic pain, love it and cuddle it and you'll see how it starts to diminish. What is your body trying to tell you through that pain?*

299. *Become an observer of your own body from inside. Quiet down and go inside yourself, teach this to your patients. Scan your body with your mind and listen to what your body has to say to you. Any area that feels stranger than the other? If your body could talk what would it be telling you?....That's right. What have you become aware of ......now?*

300. *Remember we all have possibilities to expand, to change and to adapt to any event.*

301. *If you see yourself as a failure that's what you would become, that's what others would perceive about you.*

302. *Self esteem is something you have to work on, nobody was born with it. It is an inside job.*

303. *The more you look for things that you don't like about someone the more you will find. Stop looking as you are only hurting yourself.*

304. *The more you can teach Heath Professionals to take care of themselves, the most cost effective it is as then you have a model of interactive medicine instead an autopilot Health Service delivery.*

305. *Every move you make, every smile you offer, every word you say has a thought behind that started it.*

306. *Help your patients to help themselves. It empowers them, boosts their immune system and makes you feel great too.*

307. *Listen to your heart before you head intervenes, then gather all the information and make the decisions.*

308. *Focus on your own growth as a person and don't compare with others. Your self growth is a present for your patients and your colleagues too.*

309. *You don't need anybody in order to forgive yourself.*

310. *Make peace with stress, this will reduce the impact it has on you and it will start to vanish.*

311. *When you have an emotional challenge presented in front of you ask yourself in silence. What kind of need lives inside me that is not being met right now?*

312. *Stretch your vocabulary and include frequently positive words like beautiful, amazing, lovely etc... Dare to use them more often and observe how you start to see more beautiful, amazing and lovely things happening to you.*

313. *In order to be accepted you have to first accept others.*

314. *Choose new empowering beliefs that uplift yourself, your patients and your colleagues.*

315. *Love and forgiveness are very healing acts.*

316. *Your first role as a health professional is to be peaceful yourself. You get to choose if you wish to practice peace or stress at work. Having peaceful thoughts opens the door to a much more productive relationship with your patients. You will transmit peace to your patients, reducing distress and opening the door to a positive engaging of your patient's mind*

317. *Unfortunately the bullying culture is still prominent within the medical profession. You may feel the need to bully a member of staff. Probably you have even been very well trained within the system to bully another and it feels as if it's your turn. Think what it is that is lacking inside yourself that is prompting you to bully someone. What exactly is the weakness you can't cope with?*

318. *Drink plenty of water to help to eliminate all those toxins that affect your mood. Choose herbal teas over coffee for the break in the ward round.*

319. *Catch that painful thought inside your head, write it down and start to challenge it with questions. Where is that thought coming from? Did I create it? Is it something someone said to me? Is that thought true? What else do I think is different from that thought?*

320. *Slow down while you eat even if it feels as if you don't have time to have your lunch. Eat slowly and give time to your body to assimilate all the nutrients from your food. Your body knows how to keep the homeostatic state better than anybody else. Allow it to do it.*

321. *You should.......you shouldn't......you have to ......you haven't ....you must.......you mustn't ....are words that automatically bring a negative feeling, a sense of something you've done wrong even before you know what it is. Don't talk to yourself on those terms. Change it to you may........ you can....... you could......*

322. *When we are babies we can move from fear to bliss in less than a minute. As babies we let the emotion go and resolve by itself. As we grow we tend to forget about how we did this and we keep the emotional states for longer, sometimes for years, entertaining the same thought over and over again.*

323. *Did you know that catecholamine levels (stress hormones) are higher in "Takotsubo Cardiomyopathy" or "Broken Heart Syndrome" than in Miocardial Infartion (heart attack)? (Wittstein, 2005) We knew this for a long time, we just didn't put it into scientific language. How many other dis......eases, dis........orders are we missing because we narrow our minds to pay attention to only evidence based literature? Keeping our curiosity open is a good way to progress towards new understanding of dis.... ease.*

324. *Wake up to the impact of your thoughts in your life. Be mindful of the consequences of your beliefs. Are they helpful to you or your patients? Are they holding you or your patients back?*

325. *Whatever emotion you put in the space between you and the rest of the staff that's exactly the emotion that will come back to you.*

326. *Self esteem is about relying on your inner being and intuition teaches you to trust your inner being.*

327. *Do you feel deep........ pressed ?...........That's right......maybe is time to start by deep ...... pleasing yourself.*

328. *We believe we are individual because we have separated bodies, but we wouldn't survive on our own.*

329. *When your body is telling you that you need to go to the loo, listen to it and make it a priority, otherwise it will affect your mood as you will be retaining toxins and absorbing them for longer.*

330. *Have you noticed that when only your ego survives you don't feel fulfilled? That's because your ego is just a part inside you and not the biggest one. Don't neglect the spiritual part of yourself as can give you many answers to practical everyday's problems too.*

331. *When your aim in life is limited to just getting through the day......that's the warning sign to start to apply urgent intensive self care.*

332. *There's a chance that genetic defects can be overridden by the environment. Think of how many different ways you can modify your environment at the work place.*

333. *If you feel threatened by the new generation of younger health professionals, remember that we are all needed. Young professionals think quicker but experienced professionals think deeper and wider. By teaching them you also absorb their energy and you settle your knowledge.*

334. *Good emotional health depends on your power to say "No" to the experiences that lead you to anger.*

335. *See your patient as a person, not only as a clinical case. Try to focus on some good qualities he may have and mention them to him. This contributes to better rapport.*

336. *Be sure that if you have practised the skill of putting yourself down and have become successful, you may as well start practising pulling yourself up and become successful too.*

337. *Pay attention to that emotion. How does it feel in your body? What is that emotion trying to tell you?*

338. *Research shows that parental love enhances brain development in children. Guess what love can do to adults too.*

339. *Start counting your blessings ....even the ones you took for granted.*

340. *Be selfish and be aware that when you are not feeling well you are probably not the best help your patients may have. Take care of yourself first.*

341. *If your heart could start singing what would it be about?*

342. *Breath in plenty of oxygen, take deep breaths. We need it to metabolise all the toxins we may have swallowed.*

343. *Keep your mind in the quiet for a bit everyday especially before going to sleep. It is then when the most inspiring thoughts come through.*

344. *Ask your patients "How does it feel in your body..........?" It can be a medication they are taken or a symptom they are having........ Feeling a symptom is different to describing it.*

345. *Someone told you as a child you were not smart enough? Smart for what exactly? There's many ways and areas for being smart. How long have you been carrying that idea around? Remember it was not your idea to start with , it was another person's idea according to how they saw their world. Your views about the world may be different.*

346. *Sometimes all it's needed inside the theatre is just a member of the staff confessing he has faith on things evolving positively for the rest of the staff to overcome their fear to allow faith to make a miracle on their behalf. What would happen if you dare to say you have faith even when you still doubt about it? Would the others expand it for you too?*

347. *Who you are goes beyond what you have or what you achieve or what other people think of you.*

348. *Question your assumptions, particularly the ones that are painful. You may be pleasantly surprised.*

349. *You become emotionally free once you find calm deep within yourself in that isle of you.*

350. *Remember that from a window you can only see a tiny little bit of sky. You have to go outside to appreciate that there's more than what you are actually seeing*

351. *You have to say thank you to be happy and not to wait to be happy to start saying thank you. It works the other way round people usually think. Try it for yourself and observe what happens.*

352. *When the work environment is psychologically healthy that improves efficiency, recruitment and retention of staff and productivity.*

353. *For how long is your mind in the future? How long is your mind in the past? And as you are ....now ......fully considering .... Where are you...... now.......?.......That's right.*

354. *Choose how you want to act in a situation instead of reacting. Make a conscious choice that supports a balanced mind and a healthy body.*

355. *If you feel agitated, ask yourself " If this agitation would have to leave my body now what way would it go ?".....That's right. Now focus on it leaving your body... push it far away from your body. Can you feel how it leaves your body?..... That's right.*

356. *Today I make the decision to live in the present. I can't see my past as I'm not looking back, I can't see fully my future as I'm making it in this precise moment. My future depends on how I feel and what I do at this precise moment.*

357. *Look around now and write all the things that are going well in your life and you didn't perceive before.*

358. *Thoughts create physiological reactions and even specific body postures, body language and muscle contractions or relaxation. But it also happens the other way round. By changing your body posture your thoughts match it. Are you lack of energy? Shake your body and see how you can self generate energy.*

359. *One of the best self care attitudes is "Silence". Silence in your mind. Discover the joy of a resting mind. Not thinking is easier than pushing yourself to think positive. If you try to think positive and it seems hard, just observe your thoughts passing by until they gradually move to slow motion and eventually stop.*

360. *Coping doesn't remove stress. Coping is stress, it means you are learning how to deal with the pain, but the pain and the stress remains and carries on damaging the body. Don't fight reality, just accept it and focus on how you would like the situation to be different and observe what happens. As your thinking moves away from the problem, reality starts to change.*

361. *In "Resuscitation and Life Support" training we learn "Look, Listen and Feel" for signs of life for 10 seconds. "Look, Listen and Feel" for signs of life in nature around you for at least 10 seconds everyday and see what difference that makes to your mood.*

362. *Choose how you respond to stress. Decide to observe it and then release it.*

363. *Life is much more than an accumulation of tasks to do.*

364. *Don't engage in unproductive negative thinking, it doesn't make you feel any good. Once you are aware of how it makes you feel it's easier to decide to move towards more positive thinking as you'll realise how the more positive thoughts feel in your body.*

365. *If you don't feel great right now that's because you are in transition towards something better. Embrace this moment as it's only change and it's always in all ways for the better.*

366. *Welcome your negative torturing thoughts, appreciate them because they tell you there's something you don't like and then wave them good bye as they have already done their purpose of informing you that you would like things being different. And from this point be determined to think what you would like instead and dream about it being awake.*

Lightning Source UK Ltd.
Milton Keynes UK
UKOW052121240113

205280UK00001B/12/P